Music, Moods and Memories
Lounge Favorites

Project Manager: Tony Esposito
Cover Illustration and Design: Joseph Klucar

© 1997 WARNER BROS. PUBLICATIONS
All Rights Reserved

BLUE TANGO

Words by
MITCHELL PARISH

Music by
LEROY ANDERSON

♦ Guitar chords
♦♦ Ukulele chord diagrams

Blue Tango - 2 - 1

Blue Tango - 2 - 2

CARA MIA

Original Words and Music by
TULIO TRAPANI and LEE LANGE

Cara Mia - 2 - 1

DO IT AGAIN

Words by
B.G. DeSYLVA

Music by
GEORGE GERSHWIN

Tell me, tell me, what did you do to me? I just got a thrill that was new to me, When your two lips were pressed to mine. When you held me,

Do It Again - 4 - 1

AMOR
(Amor, Amor, Amor)

English Words by NORMAN NEWELL
Spanish Words by RICARDO LOPEZ MENDEZ

Music by GABRIEL RUIZ

A - mor, a - mor, a - mor
A - mor, a - mor, a - mor,

that's how I say the lat - in way how much I love you
Na - cio de ti, Na - cio de mi, de la es - pe - ran - za

A - mor, a - mor, a - mor,
A - mor, a - mor, a - mor,

Amor - 3 - 1

12

Amor - 3 - 3

MOONGLOW

Words and Music by
WILL HUDSON, EDDIE DE LANGE
and IRVING MILLS

Moonglow - 3 - 1

14

Moonglow - 3 - 2

Moonglow - 3 - 3

From the Warner Bros. Motion Picture "CASABLANCA"

AS TIME GOES BY

Words and Music by
HERMAN HUPFELD

As Time Goes by - 4 - 1

18

SIBONEY

American Lyric by
DOLLY MORSE

Spanish Lyric and Music by
ERNESTO LECUONA

If you've been _____ in Ha - van - a _____ You have
Si - bo - ney _____ yo te quie - ro yo me

heard a dream-y tune, _____ When you think _____ of Ha-
mue - ro por tu a - mor _____ Si - bo - ney _____ en tu

Siboney - 4 - 1

Chorus, Moderato

Si- bo - ney, _____ that's the tune that_ they croon at you down Ha-van-a way, _____
Si - bo - ney _____ *de mi sue - ño si no a - yes la que - ja de mi voz* _____

Si - bo - ney, _____ that's the
Si - bo - ney _____ *si no*

dance that_ they_ dance at_ the Ca - fé, _____
vie - nes me mo - ri - ré de a - mor _____

And that tune _____ brings_you dreams so_ it seems un - der-neath the
Si - bo - ney _____ *de mi sue - ño te es - pe - ro con an - sia en*

YOU BELONG TO MY HEART
(Solamente Una Vez)

English Lyrics by
RAY GILBERT

Spanish Lyrics and Music by
AGUSTIN LARA

You Belong to My Heart - 2 - 1

You Belong to My Heart - 2 - 2

GEORGIA ON MY MIND

Lyric by
STUART GORRELL

Music by
HOAGY CARMICHAEL

Georgia on My Mind - 3 - 1

28

BESAME MUCHO

English Lyric by
SUNNY SKYLAR

Music and Spanish Lyric by
CONSUELO VELAZQUEZ

Besame Mucho - 3 - 1

NIGHT AND DAY

French Version by
EMELIA RENAUD

Words and Music by
COLE PORTER

Moderato

mp poco a poco cresc.

Like the beat, beat, beat, of the tom-tom; When the jun-gle shad-ows
Com-me le rou-le-ment du tam-tam, Quand la jon-gle s'ob-scur-

fall, Like the tick, tick, tock of the state-ly clock, as it stands a-gainst the
cit, Com-me le tic-tac de l'hor-lo-ge ma-jes-tu-eu-se près du

wall, Like the drip, drip, drip, of the rain-drops, When the sum-mer show'r is
mur Com-me la gout-te d'eau qui tom-be Quand un o-rage est fi-

Night and Day - 4 - 1

34

JUST ONE OF THOSE THINGS

Words and Music by
COLE PORTER

38

BLUE MOON

Lyric by
LORENZ HART

Music by
RICHARD RODGERS

Ab6 Bb7 Eb Ab6 Bb7
sud - den - ly ap - peared be - fore me The on - ly one my arms will ev - er
Eb Abm 4 fr. Db9 Gb
Hold, I heard some - bod - y whis - per, "Please a - dore me," And when I
Bb F7 Fm7 Bb7 Eb Cm Fm7 Bb7
looked, the moon had turned to gold! Blue Moon now I'm no long - er a - lone
Eb Cm Fm Bb7 Eb Cm Fm7
With - out a dream in my heart, With - out a love of my own.
1. 2.
Eb Ab 4 fr. Eb Bb7 Eb Ab6 Eb
mf
Blue
rit. e dim.

WHATEVER LOLA WANTS
(Lola Gets)

Words and Music by
RICHARD ADLER and
JERRY ROSS

Whatever Lola Wants (Lola Gets) - 3 - 1

44

Whatever Lola Wants (Lola Gets) - 3 - 3

RUBY

Words by
MITCHELL PARISH

Music by
HEINZ ROEMHELD

TICO TICO
(Tico Tico No Fuba)

Portuguese Lyrics by
ALOYSIO OLIVEIRA
English Lyrics by ERVIN DRAKE

Music by ZEQUINHA ABREU

Tico Tico - 4 - 1

Tico Tico - 4 - 2

TI - CO - TI - CO TI - CO-TI - CO tock. Oh, TI-CO tock.___ tock.
bá é que é bo-a a - li-men-ta- ção. O ti-co ção.___ ção.___

Interlude

mp   sfz

Tico Tico - 4 - 4   D. S. al Fine

SINCE I FELL FOR YOU

Words and Music by
BUDDY JOHNSON

When you just give love and nev- er get love You'd bet- ter let love de- part.

I know it's so and yet I know— I can't get you out of my heart.—

You ———— made me leave my hap-py home, ———— You took my love and now you're

gone ———— SINCE I — FELL FOR YOU.—

SHANGRI-LA

Lyrics by
CARL SIGMAN

Music by
MATT MALNECK and
ROBERT MAXWELL

SINCERELY

Words and Music by
ALLAN FREED and
HARVEY FUQUA

Sincerely - 3 - 1

58

SKYLARK

Words by
JOHNNY MERCER

Music by
HOAGY CARMICHAEL

Skylark - 3 - 1

THE BOULEVARD OF BROKEN DREAMS

Words by
AL DUBIN

Music by
HARRY WARREN

*Diagrams for Guitar, Symbols for Ukulele and Banjo

The Boulevard of Broken Dreams - 3 - 1

REFRAIN

CANADIAN SUNSET

Music by
EDDIE HEYWOOD

Moderately, With A Good Beat

Canadian Sunset - 3 - 1

Canadian Sunset - 3 - 3

IT'S ONLY A PAPER MOON

Words by
BILLY ROSE and
E. Y. HARBURG

Music by
HAROLD ARLEN

It's Only a Paper Moon - 4 - 2

It's Only a Paper Moon - 4 - 3

It's Only a Paper Moon - 4 - 4

SOMETHING'S GOTTA GIVE

Words and Music by
JOHNNY MERCER

Something's Gotta Give - 4 - 1

SATIN DOLL

Words and Music by
JOHNNY MERCER, DUKE ELLINGTON
and BILLY STRAYHORN

Satin Doll - 2 - 1

QUIEN SERA
(Sway)

English Words by
NORMAN GIMBEL

Spanish Words and Music by
PABLO BELTRAN RUIZ

Quien Sera - 2 - 1

TAKING A CHANCE ON LOVE

Words by
JOHN LATOUCHE and
TED FETTER

Music by
VERNON DUKE

Taking A Chance On Love - 2 - 1

81

Taking A Chance On Love - 2 - 2

PATRICIA

Words by
BOB MARCUS

Music by
PEREZ PRADO

Patricia - 4 - 1

Patricia - 4 - 2

84

Patricia - 4 - 3

PERFIDIA

English Lyrics by
MILTON LEEDS

Words and Music by
ALBERTO DOMINGUEZ

Perfidia - 4 - 1

Perfidia - 4 - 2

88

Perfidia - 4 - 3

OYE COMO VA

Words and Music by
TITO PUENTE

Oye Como Va - 2 - 1

Oye Como Va - 2 - 2

BETWEEN THE DEVIL AND THE DEEP BLUE SEA

Words by
TED KOEHLER

Music by
HAROLD ARLEN

what can I do? I don't know what makes me string a - long.

CHORUS

I don't want you, but I'd hate to lose you, You've got me

in be-tween __ the de-vil and the deep blue sea, __ I for-

give you, 'cause I can't for- get you, You've got me in be-tween __ the

de-vil and the deep blue sea, ___ I ought to cross you off my list, ___ but when you come knocking

at my door, ___ Fate seems to give my heart a twist, and I come run-ning back for

more, I should hate you, but I guess I love you,

You've got me in be-tween ___ the de-vil and the deep blue sea. ___ ___

CUTE

Words by
STANLEY STYNE

Music by
NEAL HEFTI

*May be sung as solo or duet

Cute - 3 - 1

Cute - 3 - 3

MAMBO NO. 5

By
PEREZ PRADO

Mambo No. 5 - 2 - 1

(Kaem Coro)

Si Si Si yo qui -ero

mf

1. 2. 3. 4.

Mam - bo!

MAMBO

mf ff

1. 2. 3. 4.

ff

Mambo No. 5 - 2 - 2

MAMBO NO. 8

By
PEREZ PRADO

Mambo No. 8 - 2 - 1

NICE 'N' EASY

Words by
ALAN and MARILYN BERGMAN

Music by
LEW SPENCE

Nice 'N' Easy - 2 - 1

HEY THERE

Words and Music by
RICHARD ADLER and
JERRY ROSS

Symbols for Guitar, Diagrams for Ukulele.

Hey There - 2 - 1

BUTTON UP YOUR OVERCOAT

Words and Music by B.G. DE SYLVA,
LEW BROWN and RAY HENDERSON

Button up Your Overcoat - 3 - 1

108

DEEP PURPLE
(Sombre Demijour)

Lyric by
MITCHELL PARISH

Music by
PETER DE ROSE

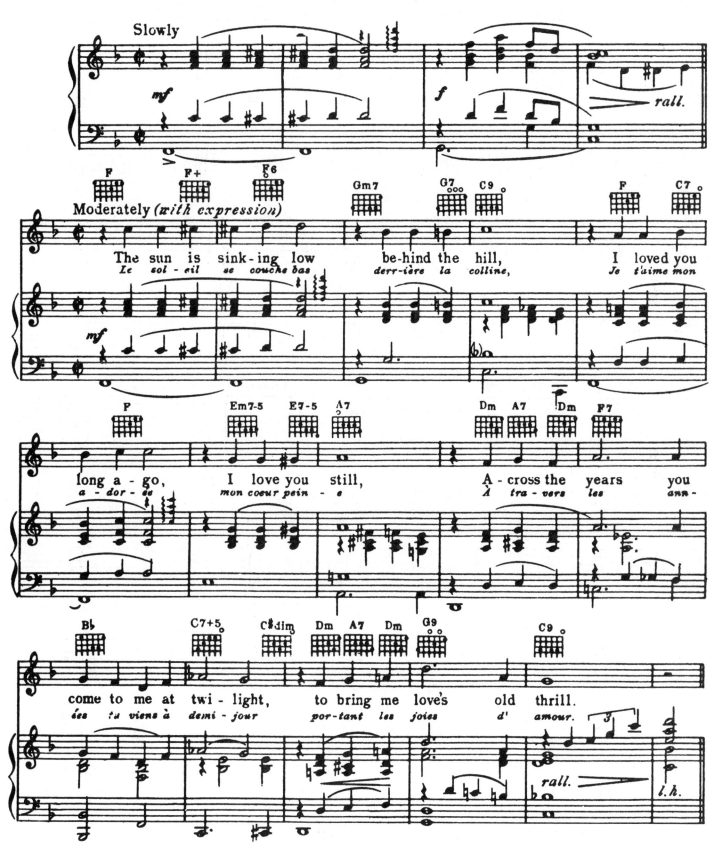

Deep Purple - 3 - 1

110

Deep Purple - 3 - 2

Deep Purple - 3 - 3

IF I LOVE AGAIN

Words by
J.P. MURRAY

Music by
BEN OAKLAND

I of-ten won-der why you came to me,___ Brought such a flame to me ___ then let it

die. And if an-oth-er love should find my heart,___ It will re-

If I Love Again - 4 - 1

114

I GET A KICK OUT OF YOU

Words and Music by
COLE PORTER

FRENESI

English Lyrics by
RAY CHARLES and
S.K. RUSSELL

Spanish Words and Music by
ALBERTO DOMINGUEZ

Frenesi - 4 - 1

123

Frenesi - 4 - 4

CARAVAN

Lyric by
IRVING MILLS

Music by
DUKE ELLINGTON,
and JUAN TIZOL

Moderato quasi misterioso

mp - mf

Ebdim C7   Ebdim. C7   Ebdim C7   Ebdim C7

Night _____ and stars a - bove that shine so

p - f

Ebdim C7   Ebdim C7   Ebdim C7   Ebdim C   Ebdim C7

bright _____ The mys-'try of their fad-ing light ___

Ebdim C7   Ebdim C7   Ebdim C7   Fm6

that shines up - on our CAR-A-VAN; ___

Caravan - 4 - 1

126

I CAN'T GET STARTED

Words by
IRA GERSHWIN

Music by
VERNON DUKE

I'm a glum one, it's ex-plain-a-ble: I met some one un-at-tain-a-ble;

Life's a bore, The world is my oy-ster no more.

I Can't Get Started - 4 - 1

CHANCES ARE

Words by
AL STILLMAN

Music by
ROBERT ALLEN

DAY BY DAY

Words and Music by
SAMMY CAHN, AXEL STORDAHL
and PAUL WESTON

Moderately Slow (*with expression*)

DAY BY DAY _____ I'm fall - ing more in love with you And

DAY BY DAY _____ my love seems to grow, _____ There

is - n't an - y end to my de - vo - tion, _____ It's

Day by Day - 2 - 1

IT'S ALL IN THE GAME

Words by
CARL SIGMAN

Music by
GEN. CHARLES G. DAWES

Slowly

Man - y a tear has to fall, but it's all in the

game. _____ All in the won-der-ful game that we know as

It's All in the Game - 3 - 1

THE GOOD LIFE

Words by
JACK REARDON

Music by
SACHA DISTEL

The Good Life - 3 - 1

FEELINGS
(¿Dime?)
Ballad

Spanish Lyrics by
THOMAS FUNDORA

English Words and Music by
LOUIS GASTE and MORRIS ALBERT

Feel - ings, ___ noth - ing more than feel - ings, ___
¿Di - me? ___ *¿so - la - men - te di - me?* ___

try - ing to for - get my feel - ings of
¿Co - mo ol - vi - dar mis sen - ti - mien - tos de a -

love. Tear-drops ___
mor? *Lá - gri - mas* ___

Feelings - 5 - 1

Feelings - 5 - 2

Feelings - 5 - 4

TOO CLOSE FOR COMFORT

Words and Music by
JERRY BOCK,
LARRY HOLOFCENER and GEORGE DAVID WEISS

148

Too Close for Comfort - 5 - 2

THE ENCHANTED SEA

By FRANK METIS
and RANDY STARR

Enchanted Sea - 2 - 1

153

Enchanted Sea - 2 - 2

THE GLOW WORM

Modern Version by
JOHNNY MERCER
Original Words by
LILLA CAYLEY ROBINSON

Music by
PAUL LINCKE

I'LL SEE YOU IN MY DREAMS

Words by
GUS KAHN

Music by
ISHAM JONES

I'll See You in My Dreams - 2 - 1

157

I'll See You in My Dreams - 2 - 2

EBB TIDE

Lyric by
CARL SIGMAN

Music by
ROBERT MAXWELL

Ebb Tide - 3 - 1

159

Ebb Tide - 3 - 2

160